Candy
Bouquets

65
50

For Celebrations!

Create Your Own Gifts & Centerpieces

Delicious Designs

Printed in the United States of America
by G&R Publishing Co.

Published By:

507 Industrial Street
Waverly, IA 50677

ISBN-13: 978-1-56383-342-7
ISBN-10: 1-56383-342-5
Item #3625

Table of Contents

Getting Started

Celebrations are even sweeter with a candy bouquet centerpiece or gift. Whether decorating for a holiday party or giving a gift to commemorate a special occasion, your friends and family will be impressed by your candy creations. The celebration suggestions, tips and variations, step-by-step instructions, illustrations, and inspiring photos on the following pages will have you searching for a reason to celebrate with a candy bouquet today.

Food Safety

Before you begin assembling candy bouquets, thoroughly wash your hands, container or base, and all utensils with soap and warm water. Although some of these items may not touch candy directly, it is best to practice safety.

Ingesting Styrofoam can be dangerous to one's health. When using Styrofoam as a base for an arrangement, always use wrapped candy. Styrofoam dust or particles can attach to candy when arranging your bouquet so it's best to make sure candy is covered before you begin. If unwrapped candy is used, it is best to use an edible base such as Crispy Marshmallow Treats (see p. 5), Kool-Aid Playdough (see p. 19), or a vase filled with candy or sugar (see p. 20 and p. 48). If you must use Styrofoam near unwrapped candy, wrap it well with plastic wrap or aluminum foil before use.

General Supplies

Common supplies used to make candy bouquets include Styrofoam, pins and a hot glue gun.

Some bouquet instructions indicate the exact size of Styrofoam piece needed for assembly because the base or container size is specific. Others are not specific because containers chosen may vary in size and it is easier to trim or cut a piece of Styrofoam to fit.

Instructions on these pages include the use of both straight pins and quilters T-pins. Although straight pins are sometimes recommended based on the final look or proper assembly of the product, the use of T-pins is generally recommended as they are stronger, more durable and larger/safer for use around food. In either case, be sure to instruct gift recipients or guests to use caution, especially when straight pins have been used.

Hot glue guns, which are available in high- and low-temperature, are very useful when making candy bouquets. Although they are sometimes interchangeable, a low-temperature glue gun is especially recommended for use with candy to avoid melting wrappers or the candy itself.

Candy and Base Materials

Most candy and base materials (as well as other supplies) can be purchased at local supermarkets, discount stores or craft stores. Seasonal candy and wrapper colors may be found at different times of the year. For example, find pastel-colored candy during the spring season or fall-colored candy for use during the autumn season.

In addition to specific suggestions on the following pages, a number of interesting, economical items can be used as bases such as gift bags, or cardboard or paper-craft boxes that have been painted, decoupaged or covered with gift wrap. Don't forget to check garage sales and thrift stores for inexpensive bases.

Be Creative

Whether making the bouquets suggested on these pages, or developing your own arrangements, it is fun to add creative twists. Be creative with coordinated or themed candy colors, names, packaging shapes and flavors. When choosing containers, think seasonally or by the theme of your bouquet and choose colors that complement each other. Find ribbon or other embellishments that bring out less prominent colors and enhance themes.

Spice it up by including various edibles or non-edibles in your arrangements, such as beef jerky, peanuts and chips for salt-lovers, band-aids in a get-well bouquet, or show tickets tucked into a candy bouquet gift.

Crispy Marshmallow Treats

Ingredients
¼ C. margarine
1 (10 oz.) bag large marshmallows (approx. 40 pcs.)
6 C. crispy cereal, such as fruity crisps or rice crisps

Instructions
Melt margarine in a large saucepan over low heat. Add marshmallows, stirring constantly, until completely melted; remove from heat. Add cereal and stir until evenly combined. Using a greased spatula, press mixture evenly into a greased 9 x 13″ baking dish, or shape as directed in candy bouquet instructions.

Sweets you will need:

- 48 (.49 oz.) Hershey's Milk Chocolate snack size bars
- 60 cinnamon disc candies (just under 1 lb.)
- 3 Sweet Stripes soft mint candy sticks
  (or old-fashioned candy sticks)
- 6 Hershey's Kisses

Supplies you will need:

- 1 (9 x 2½″) pc. round Styrofoam (or use two 1¼″ pieces)
- Aluminum foil
- 12″ pedestal glass cake plate
- Poster putty
- Low-temperature hot glue gun

- Double stick tape
- Clear cellophane, optional
- Clear tape, optional
- Craft wire or twist ties
- 3 (2 x 5″) pcs. red cellophane
- 3 (2 x 5″) pcs. yellow cellophane
- 3 toothpicks

To Begin...

1 Wrap the Styrofoam base in aluminum foil. Secure foil wrapped Styrofoam to the cake plate with poster putty.

2 Place two dots of hot glue on the back side (seam side) of a Hershey's bar and press against Styrofoam base. Continue to glue candy bars around the base making sure all wrapper writing faces the same direction. Using the hot glue gun, secure the top edge of each wrapper to the top of the base by folding it over onto a dot of hot glue.

3 Secure cinnamon disc candies along the base of the cake plate with small pieces of double stick tape. Fasten a cinnamon disc to bottom right hand corner of each of the remaining Hershey's bars, with a

continued

small piece of double stick tape. Lay Hershey's/discs around the top, in a "fanned" pattern. Leave an empty circle at the center of the "cake." (Glue or tape is not required for the top of the cake but is optional to secure for transport.)

4 If using wrapped candy sticks, skip to step 5. Roll unwrapped candy sticks in clear cellophane and seal the seam with clear tape. Twist ends and secure with craft wire.

5 Lay a piece of red cellophane over a piece of yellow cellophane and work the bottom edges into a gathered bunch. Secure it with craft wire to the twisted top of a candy stick to create a "lit candle."

6 Tape a toothpick to the base of the candle and insert it into the top of the cake. Sprinkle extra cinnamon disc candies and Hershey's Kisses to fill the center of the cake.

Celebration Suggestions...

Happy Birthday! Remove candles and top with additional Kisses and cinnamon discs to say, "Happy Anniversary," "Farewell," or to serve as part of a Dinner Party Dessert Buffet.

Sweets you will need:

1 (750 ml) wine bottle
8 to 12 Lindt Lindor Truffles
(or chocolates with twisted wrapper ends)

- **Gold craft wire (24 gauge)**
- **Wire snips**

- **Assorted beads, colors coordinated with wine bottle and truffle wrappers**

To Begin...

1 Measure bottle height. Cut a piece of craft wire 10″ longer than the height of the bottle, as this will allow for twists of beads to curl above the bottle. Fasten one bead onto one end of the wire. String beads onto wire in a random pattern until wire has 3 to 4″ bare. Twist one bead onto the other end of the wire so beads will not fall off. (The bare space on wire will make it easier to twist wire around the top of the bottle later.)

2 To attach candy to loosely beaded wire, slide 2 to 4 inches worth of beads to one end. Twist the bare wire around the loose end of one truffle wrapper. Slide several more inches of beads against the first truffle and attach a second truffle to the wire. Repeat to add a third.

3 Slide approximately 4 to 5″ of beads taut against the top end of the wire. Carefully wind the bare wire around the top of the wine bottle, along with a few of the loosely strung beads for visual interest. Twist wires together tightly to secure. Slide approximately 4 to 5″ of beads against the top end of the wire. Twist the beaded wires around fingers to create "curls." Repeat these steps to add 2 or 3 more strings of beads with 2 to 3 truffles each.

4 To add additional "curls" of beads above the bottle, cut 2 wires approximately 12″ in length and string losely with beads. Wind the center bare portion of each beaded wire around the top of the bottle and twist to secure. Twist to "curl" the ends. Trim excess wire as needed.

Celebration Suggestions...

Anniversary, New Year's Celebration, Valentine's Day, Engagement, Wedding, Hostess Gift, Housewarming or Job Promotion.

A Sweetheart of a Bouquet

Sweets you will need:

24 Hershey's Kisses
18 Andes Mints
6 rolls mint-flavored (white) Mentos

Supplies you will need:

- Double stick tape
- 16 (6 x 8") pcs. red cellophane
- 17 (18") wire floral stems, 16 to 18 guage (16 gauge recommended)
- Green floral tape
- 18 (4 x 6") pcs. green cellophane
- 15 (6 x 6") pcs. clear plastic food wrap
- 15 (4") green chenille stems
- Glass bud vase (approx. 9" tall) with a bow
- Wire snips
- Additional green cellophane, optional
- Craft wire, optional

To Begin...

1 Fasten the flat sides of two Hershey's Kisses together with a small piece of double stick tape. Fold a piece of red cellophane so the 8" sides meet; lay the double Kiss inside, with a small margin between the fold and candy. Roll the Kisses from one edge to the other at a slight angle, allowing the folded edge to roll lower around the outside of the "bud."

2 Twist the cellophane at the bottom of the bud and wind it around one end of a floral stem. While holding the bud and stem tightly with one hand, wrap floral tape around both to secure together; continue to wind tape down the stem about 3" and then set aside.

3 Fold a piece of green cellophane so the 4″ sides meet; lay an Andes Mint inside, with a small margin between the fold and the candy. Fold each side of cellophane to the back of the mint to form a pointed tip; then fold back remaining cellophane to form a "leaf." Twist at the bottom and secure the leaf to the stem, with floral tape where floral tape left off in step 2. Continue to wind tape around remainder of stem.

4 Repeat steps 1 through 3 to complete 12 roses; on half, include 2 Andes Mint leaves.

5 Place 5 unwrapped Mentos in the center of a piece of clear food wrap, pull the corners up above the center and twist tightly.* Hold wrapped Mentos and a floral stem tightly in one hand and with your other hand, tightly wind a chenille stem to fasten them together. Leave the last 1″ of chenille loose to begin floral tape; wrap the next 2″ of stem with tape, then twist loose end of chenille over tape-wrapped stem.

6 Add two more Mentos bundles to the stem with the same method; wrap remainder of stem with floral tape. Repeat steps 5 & 6 to make 5 stems of "baby's breath."

7 Arrange all stems in the vase; with the wire snips, trim a few stems by 2 to 3″ for height variety in the arrangement. If desired, tuck green cellophane into the edge of the vase to hide the stems.

Tip: Handling sticky floral tape can cause fingerprint marks on cellophane. As an option, wrap all buds and leaves at once, twisting ends with small pieces of craft wire to secure before fastening to stems.

*Wash hands thoroughly before handling unwrapped food.

Celebration Suggestions...

Valentine's Day, Birthday, Anniversary, Wedding Shower, Mother's Day or just say, "I love you!"

Sweets you will need:

- 4 to 5 mini Spree candy rolls
- 4 to 5 hard candy discs in bright, solid-colored wrappers
- 6 Laffy Taffy ropes (1 each of yellow, green, orange, blue, red and purple)
- 25 to 30 milk chocolate gold coins
- ¾ to 1 lb. assorted green jelly beans
- Blue cotton candy

Supplies you will need:

- Low-temperature hot glue gun
- 4 to 5 (¼ x 5½″) green wood craft sticks, cut in half
- 8 to 10 (5″) pcs. green shamrock wire garland
- Kool-Aid Playdough*, see recipe p. 19
- Double stick tape
- Wire coat hanger, hook removed and trimmed to 12″

- Clear tape
- Glass "pot" (large votive candle holder, approx. 3 x 3″), remove any labels
- 1 (1½ x 1½ x 1¼″) pc. Styrofoam
- High-temperature hot glue gun
- Glass luncheon/tea plate (approx. 6 x 10″)

To Begin...

1 With a low-temperature hot glue gun, glue a Spree candy roll to a craft stick so that half the roll is positioned halfway onto the stick; repeat with remaining Sprees. Using the hot glue again, adhere a wrapped candy disc to a craft stick with a dot of glue. Repeat with remaining candy discs. Twist a piece of wire garland around each stick.

2 Roll playdough into 1″ balls. Insert the end of each glued candy-stick into the ball and pinch dough up around the stick with both thumbs and forefingers, creating a base for each "flower." Dry for 12 hours upright, then 12 hours laying on their sides.

17

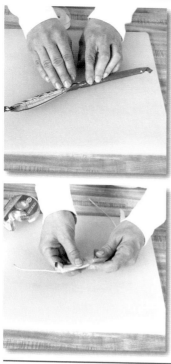

3 For each taffy, fold seam over to reveal plain flap; use double stick tape to secure flap flat. Gently bend yellow taffy and wire hanger to form an arc. Use clear tape to fasten the wire to the writing side of the taffy; the plain flap should be on the front side of the rainbow. Leave 2″ of wire exposed on the right end of the arc. Bend and tape remaining taffy to wired yellow taffy, in rainbow-color order (red, orange, yellow, green, blue, purple).

4 Use a high-temperature hot glue gun to place a generous amount of glue on a 1½ x 1¼″ side of the Styrofoam and secure in the bottom of the pot. Use a generous amount of high-temperature hot glue to secure the pot to the glass plate, in one corner. Insert wire end of rainbow into Styrofoam. Fill the pot with gold coins, positioning them to hide Styrofoam.

5 Arrange Spree and disc candy flowers on the tray. Add jelly beans to fill the tray.

6 Arrange a large fluff of cotton candy by laying it over the end of the rainbow to disguise rough end and serve as clouds.

Since Kool-Aid Playdough is made with all food ingredients, it is harmless if ingested. A substitution of purchased playdough should not be made, as jelly beans rest against it.

Celebration Suggestions...

St. Patrick's Day, Good Luck, Birthday for an Irishman or just say "There's a silver lining to every cloud, and a pot of gold at the end of every rainbow – CHEER UP!"

Kool-Aid Playdough

Ingredients

1 C. flour   1 env. Kool-Aid drink mix
½ C. salt   1 C. water
1 T. cream of tartar   1 T. cooking oil

Instructions

In a large saucepan, combine flour, salt, cream of tartar and drink mix. Slowly add water and oil and stir over medium heat until mixture thickens to dough. Turn out onto a heatproof surface, such as a bread board, and knead until smooth. When fully cooled, store in an air-tight container.

Note: For use in the base of the St. Patrick's Day candy bouquet, use lemon-lime flavor or other green colored drink mix. Allow dough to cool completely before shaping to dry.

Flower Power

Sweets you will need:

- 4 to 6 pastel Tootsie Pop suckers
- 4 to 6 pastel Rolo chocolate caramels
- 12 to 16 oz. pastel M&Ms

Supplies you will need:

- 3″ flower cookie cutter
- 6 to 8 sheets assorted scrapbooking paper
- Paper punch or X-acto knife
- 4 to 6 brass fasteners
- Low-temperature hot glue gun
- 4 to 6 (6″) chenille stems, any color
- 8 to 12 colored flexible drinking straws
- Clear glass vase (approx. 3 x 3 x 5¼″)

To Begin...

1 To make a Tootsie Pop bloom, use a flower cookie cutter to trace a pattern onto a piece of scrapbooking paper. Lay a coordinating piece of paper beneath the traced piece of paper; hold the two pieces together and carefully cut two flowers at one time.

2 With the paper punch or X-acto knife, create a hole to slide the sucker stick through. Fan out papers to show alternating colors or patterns of petals. Repeat steps to make additional flowers. Slide sucker sticks into drinking straws to complete flower stems.

3 To make a Rolo bloom, cut 10 strips of paper into even pieces, ½″ wide and 4″ to 5″ long. Make a loop with one strip of paper and push brass fastener through the matched-up ends of the loop. Continue until all 10 loops are connected, flatten the back of the fastener and fan out paper loops to create the full bloom.

4 Using the glue gun, squeeze glue onto the round part of the fastener and adhere the bottom side of a Rolo as the center of the flower. Repeat steps to make additional flowers.

5 To add stems to Rolo flowers, wrap one end of a chenille stem around the brass fastener ends on the back side of the bloom. Slide the other end of the stem inside a straw to create the full stem.

6 Fill the glass vase with M&Ms to use as an anchor for the flowers. Trim straws to create shorter stems, or tuck one straw end inside another straw end to create taller stems. Optionally, sucker sticks can be shortened slightly (cut up to 1″ from end) to allow the flex of the straw to bend, making it easier for Tootsie Pop blooms to face forward.

Celebration Suggestions...

Mother's Day, May Day, Easter, Baby Shower, Birthday or Get Well or say, "Welcome to the neighborhood!"

Sweets you will need:

- 3 100 Grand candy bars
- 5 Pay Day candy bars
- 1 (12 oz.) bag silver Hershey's Milk Chocolate Nuggets
- 10 to 12 milk chocolate coins

- Styrofam
- Large mug (approx. 5″ diameter, 3½″ tall)
- 1 (approx. 24 x 54″) pc. tulle, color coordinated with mug
- Low-temperature hot glue gun
- 12 (10″ to 12″) wood or bamboo skewers
- Pruning shears
- Play money
- Stapler
- 10 to 12 (12″) wire floral stems, 18 guage
- Wire snips

To Begin...

1 Trim Styrofoam to fit snugly into mug. Fan-fold tulle into a large square; lay foam in center and bring outsides of tulle up and around it. Tuck wrapped foam back into mug, so tulle fluffs out on each side.

2 To obtain various heights of candy bars in the arrangement, use pruning shears to trim ends of skewers before gluing to candy. (If trimmed after gluing, the pointed end will be removed, making it more difficult to insert into Styrofoam.)

3 On the back side of a 100 Grand candy bar, place a dot of hot glue on each end and lay a skewer across the hot glue dots.

4 When dry, wrap a piece of paper money around skewer; secure with stapler. Insert skewer into Styrofoam base. Repeat steps 3 and 4 with remaining 100 Grand and Pay Day bars.

5 Lay 4 silver Hershey's Nuggets face-down in a vertical line, making sure all writing will be going the appropriate direction. Place one dot of hot glue on each Nugget and lay a skewer across hot glue dots. Insert skewers into Styrofoam to arrange in the bouquet.

6 Place a dot of hot glue onto a chocolate coin and lay a floral wire into the glue. When dry, wrap a folded/fanned piece of paper money around the stem; staple to secure. To obtain various heights of coins, use a wire snips to trim wires. Insert wires into Styrofoam to arrange coins in bouquet.

Celebration Suggestions...

Thank You, Employee/Customer Appreciation or say, "You're One in a Million," for a Birthday, Job Promotion, Farewell or Congratulations.

Congratulations, You Little Smartie!

Not dum dum, or nerd
Not slow poke or air head
You rose through the grades
You're a Smartie instead –
Congrats!

Sweets you will need:

- 10 miniature boxes of Nerds
- 26 to 28 Dum Dum suckers
- 15 miniature Slo Pokes (not on sticks)
- 20 Smarties rolls
- 3 small Air Heads candies

Supplies you will need:

- Extra large mug (approx. 4″ diameter, 5″ tall)*
- Styrofoam ball, slightly larger than the mug opening
- Sharp knife
- Colored cellophane or aluminum foil
- Twist-tie or craft wire (24 to 26 gauge)
- T-pins
- 20 to 24 (¼ x 5½″) colored or natural wood craft sticks
- Clear tape
- White paper
- 1 (5 x 8″) pc. tag/poster board in school colors or black
- Double stick tape or glue
- 1 (8″ to 9″) skewer (or hot glue two craft sticks together to make a long one)
- 60″ embroidery floss in school colors
- 1 (2 x 4″) pc. tag/poster board
- 18″ to 24″ ribbon in school colors

To Begin...

1 Mark a circle on the Styrofoam ball, around the rim of the mug. Trim it to fit very snugly into the mug, with about half of the ball "mounding" above the rim. Wrap it in cellophane, secure with a twist tie on the underside and replace it in the mug, pressing down firmly.

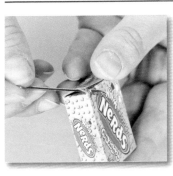

2 Insert a T-pin into open slit of a Nerds folded box lid, and poke it through the backside fold at an angle. Press the T-pin into foam so the box hangs at an angle along the mug rim. Continue until the bottom row is filled with Nerds boxes.

3 Insert sucker sticks into foam just above the row of Nerds.** Continue to tightly insert two rows of suckers.

4 Insert a T-pin through one twisted end of a Slo Poke wrapper. Add 2 more Slo Pokes to the same pin. Secure T-pin in Styrofoam above the rows of suckers. Continue to add Slo Poke candies until top of arrangement is loosely filled.

5 Fasten each Smartie and Air Head roll to a craft stick with wrapped clear tape. Arrange Air Heads as desired. Insert Smartie stick ends into Styrofoam along the top of arrangement.

6 Use the photo as a guide to create a pattern for a graduation cap; cut from tag board. Print or handwrite a message on white paper, trim slightly smaller than tag board, and mount with double stick tape. Mount cap to 8″ skewer with tape, and insert into the arrangement.

7 Fold the 4 x 2″ piece of tag board in half, to a 2 x 2″ square. Cut three 8″ lengths of embroidery floss and lay them inside, along the fold of the cardboard. Cut one 8″ piece of floss; set aside. Wind remaining floss around the folded cardboard about 12 times. Slide looped floss off cardboard; use the 3 strings from the inside folded edge to knot the loop.

8 Tie the set-aside floss around the loops, just below the first knot. Snip the bottom of looped floss to create the tassle; trim evenly. If desired, braid the 6 long ends together (in 3 pairs). Hang the tassle over the top edge of the graduation cap and secure to the back side with clear tape.

9 Create a ribbon-tied "diploma" of white paper to slide over one of the Smarties.

*Scale back candy amounts and cap and diploma sizes if using a smaller mug.

**Blunt ends of sticks can be tricky to poke through cellophane; use the tip of a knife to puncture a starter hole for sticks if necessary.

Rhyme Suggestions...

Not dum dum, or nerd
Not slow poke or air head
You rose (through the grades/to the top)
You're a Smartie instead!
Congratulations!

No longer a dum dum
Never a nerd or slow poke
You've (graduated/been promoted) now,
To be a Smartie, no joke!
Congratulations!

You're in a good crowd
With the Smarties on top
The rest may be sweet
But YOU can't be beat!
Congratulations!

Celebration Suggestions...

Graduation... or change the shape of the poem tag to celebrate the Honor Roll, School-Year End or a Job Promotion.

Fireworks Extravaganza

Sweets you will need:

- 4 env. Pop Rocks
- 16 sleeves large Sixlets
- 5 to 7 (3″) round swirl lollipops
- 3 to 5 rock candy sticks
- 5 to 7 (3″) stick swirl lollipops

Supplies you will need:

- Glass or vase (Sample is 6¾″ tall/22 oz. old-fashioned Coke glass.)
- Styrofoam
- 1 (18 x 18″) sheet red metallic foil tissue
- 7 to 9 (12″) silver chenille sparkle stems
- 3 to 5 (2″) silver chenille sparkle stems
- 7 (12″) wood or bamboo skewers
- Narrow strips of aluminum foil
- 7 to 9 (8″) pcs. of silver star wire garland
- Clear tape
- 12 silver metallic floral blades, optional
- Paring knife, optional
- Clear plastic food wrap
- 3 (8″) white lollipop/cookie sticks

To Begin...

1 Trim Styrofoam to fit in the top of the glass (approx. 3″ diameter, 2½″ tall). Set Styrofoam in the center of the foil tissue, pull corners up, gather at the center and twist with a 12″ sparkle stem to secure. Line the inside of the glass with Pop Rocks packets, slide the Styrofoam in, and trim the tissue to stand about 3″ above the top of the Styrofoam.

2 Wrap a strip of foil around a wood skewer. Join 4 Sixlets sleeves at their centers, sliding round candies evenly to the ends of the wrappers; then twist together with a piece of wire garland. Use the wire garland tails to fasten the Sixlet bunch to the top of the skewer. If desired, tape 3 silver metallic floral blades to the wood skewers so they extend beyond the Sixlets by 5″ to 6″. Repeat these steps to complete 4 Sixlets spikes. Insert the skewers into the Styrofoam.

3 Arrange the round swirl lollipops by inserting them into the Styrofoam; use the point of a knife to puncture a starter hole in foil tissue if necessary.

4 Skip to step 5 if the following does not apply. If rock candy sticks are in loose, unattractive or no packaging, wrap or re-wrap in plastic food wrap and twist the ends to close. Secure the wrapping at the top with a 2″ piece of sparkle stem. Secure the wrapping around the stick of the rock candy with a piece of wire garland; make curly loops with the tails.

5 Fasten each rock candy stick to a white lollipop/cookie stick with a 12″ sparkle stem by triple wrapping it at the top and winding the stem down the sticks so white is exposed between silver. Add rock candy sticks to the arrangement by inserting them into the styrofoam.

6 Wrap strips of aluminum foil around 3 wood skewers. Attach a stick swirl lollipop to each skewer with a 12″ sparkle stem; wind the entire stem tightly and densely around the top of the lollipop stick. Insert short and extended lollipops into the Styrofoam to complete the arrangement.

Celebration Suggestions...

Fourth of July, Congratulations, The Sky's the Limit (Good Luck), Birthday, Thank You or say, "You Color My World" or "You Light Up My Life."

Have a Ball

Sweets you will need:

- 5 Hershey's Skor candy bars
- 48 to 65 pcs. (approx. 9 oz.) foil-wrapped
  chocolate sports balls

Supplies you will need:

- **Styrofoam**
- **Sports themed container (approx. 4″ tall)**
- **White shredded crinkle paper**
- **Low-temperature hot glue gun**
- **10 wood craft sticks**
- **7 to 9 (12″) wooden or bamboo skewers**
- **Pruning shears**

To Begin...

1. Trim Styrofoam to fit snugly in the container. Cover the Styrofoam with white shredded paper. Press down gently to secure the Styrofoam and paper into the container.

2. Place hot glue along half of a wood craft stick; gently press the back of a Skor bar onto the hot glue. Repeat with remaining Skor bars.

3. Insert Skor bar sticks into the Styrofoam in a fanned pattern along the center of the container; leave room in front and behind them for sports ball candy skewers to be inserted.

4 Place a dot of hot glue on the end of a wood craft stick and adhere a chocolate sports ball to the stick. Continue to glue balls, alternating pattern and color, until 4 balls are on each of the remaining 5 sticks. Insert sticks into the Styrofoam in front of the arranged Skor bars.

5 Leaving 2 to 3 skewers at a 12″ length, trim 2″ from the remaining skewers with the pruning shears. Glue additional balls to skewers as shown with sticks in step 4, and arrange behind the Skor bars by inserting skewers into the Styrofoam.

Celebration Suggestions...

Good Luck, Birthday or Great Job – You Made the Team!
Say "Congrats on Your Top Skors" or "You Skored Big!"

Sweets you will need:

- 1 batch pink* Crispy Marshmallow Treats
  (recipe on p. 5)
- 6 candy necklaces
- 6 candy lipsticks
- 6 candy ring pops

Supplies you will need:

(for 1 bouquet crown and 6 girls' crowns)

- 2 (12 x 18″) papers for patterns
- 3 (12 x 18″) pink foam craft sheets
- 9″ glass pie plate
- 8″ to 9″ dinner plate
- X-acto knife
- Low-temperature hot glue gun
- 1 (25 yd. x 6″) roll pink tulle

- Craft wire
- Assorted embellishments
- 18 pink and/or purple flexible drinking straws
- 18 (10″) wooden or bamboo skewers
- 6 plastic headbands

To Begin...

1 Cut one piece of paper in half lengthwise, creating two 6 x 15″ narrow strips. Fold strips in half widthwise and use Diagram A (p. 39) to mark both pieces for use as patterns; cut according to diagram instructions. Overlap pattern pieces until seams are matched such that, when trimmed, a point on the crown will be formed; tape to secure. Set pie plate on top of an overturned dinner plate. Place crown pattern around the plates to ensure proper sizing, then adjust as necessary. Trim the seam corners to form a crown point. Remove tape and use the patterns to mark the foam sheet. Cut the 2 foam crown pieces.

2 Using a paper remnant from the previous pattern, make a diamond pattern using Diagram B (p. 39). Lay foam crown pieces flat on a cutting surface. Trace diamond shapes onto the points of the crown and cut them out with an X-acto knife. (Wait to cut the diamonds from the seam points until crown pieces are fastened together.) Use hot glue to secure the seams of the crown. Carefully cut diamonds from the seam points with the X-acto knife.

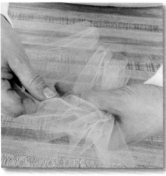

3 Place one end of a 48″ strip of tulle into the center of one palm working with fingers to gather into a bundle in the hand. Use the opposite hand to guide the tulle. Once gathered, pinch the bundle at the center and fasten with craft wire; twist to secure. Gently poke the two wire ends through the foam from the front to the inside of the crown, near the bottom edge. Pull gently to fit the tulle snugly against the crown, trim wire ends and bend them flat against the crown. Repeat to complete crown; embellish as desired. (Example uses 16 tulle tufts.)

4 Grease the pie plate with margarine. Mix up the batch of Crispy Marshmallow Treats and press into the prepared pie plate with lightly greased fingers or rubber spatula to use as the base of the arrangement.

5 Use 8″ strips of tulle to tie candy necklaces, lipsticks and ring pops to the flex ends of the straws. Trim straws to various lengths; arrange by inserting them into the base and bending the flex of the straws for desired placement.

6 Place the crown over the dinner plate and ease the filled pie plate carefully down into the center of the crown to rest evenly on the dinner plate.

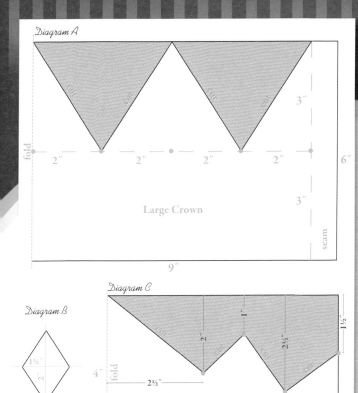

Diagram A

cut — cut — cut — cut

3″

fold

2″ — 2″ — 2″ — 2″

6″

Large Crown

3″

seam

9″

Diagram B

1⅛″

2″

Diagram C

cut — cut — cut — cut

2″

1″

2½″

1½″

fold

4″

2½″

2⅛″

Small Crown

6″

To make the little girl's crown...

Fold and cut paper for the pattern according to Diagram C. Lay pattern to mark and cut the crown from the remaining foam sheet. Trim the previously used diamond pattern to an appropriate size for the small crown. Mark, cut and remove the diamond shapes with the X-acto knife. Center the foam crown piece along the inside edge of a headband, matching the bottom edge of the foam along the headband; secure in place with hot glue. Add tulle and embellishments as described above in step 3; trim tulle tufts to desired length.

Franken Berry cereal was the pink cereal used in this recipe.

Celebration Suggestions...

Birthday, Tea or Princess Themed Party

Oh Happy Day!

Sweets you will need:

- 1¼ C. yellow vanilla flavored candy wafers
- ½ C. milk (or dark) chocolate flavored candy wafers
- 2 (2.25 oz.) pkgs. Pixy Stix (about 60 total)
- 1 to 1½ (7 oz.) boxes Gobstopper candy

Supplies you will need:

- 9 (8″) lollipop sticks
- Small plastic bag
- 2″ smiley-face candy sucker mold
- 2″ star candy sucker mold
- 9 (9 x 9″) pcs. clear cellophane or stiff wrap
- 6 (9″) pcs. colorful ribbon
- 6 (6″ to 8″) pcs. narrow rick-rack

- 1 (29 oz.) empty fruit can (approx. 4″ diameter, 4½″ tall)
- Duct tape, optional
- Styrofoam
- Aluminum foil
- 1 large rubber band
- 1 (15″) pc. wide rick-rack or ribbon
- 1 straight pin

To Begin...

1 Test the fit of 8″ sticks in the stick channels of the candy molds. If channels are too short, use a utility or X-acto knife to cut away the plastic mold, allowing the stick to extend beyond the original channel.

2 Melt yellow and milk chocolate candy wafers according to package instructions. Allow candy to cool slightly, then spoon a few tablespoons into the plastic bag. Work chocolate into one corner of the bag, and seal. Twist the bag and trim the tip from one corner. Carefully squeeze to fill smile and eye crevices of the candy molds.

3 Carefully spoon melted yellow candy over the smile and eyes to fill the cavity. Do not overfill. Lay sticks into channels so they reach to the center of the chocolate circle; rotate stick to coat. Lightly tap mold tray on work surface to release air bubbles.

4 Fill 3 star molds with melted yellow candy and 3 with melted chocolate. Add sticks so that the tips reach to the centers of the star, rotate stick to coat and tap mold gently to release air bubbles. Chill molded candy for 20 to 30 minutes or until firm. Invert mold onto a flat surface and tap gently to release. If necessary, trim edges of lollipops with a knife to make a smooth edge.

5 Lay a star lollipop on a cellophane square so the stick points toward one corner. Fold the top corner over the top to match up with the bottom corner. Gently fold cellophane towards the back to create a smooth appearance on the front of the star. Tie to secure with ribbon.

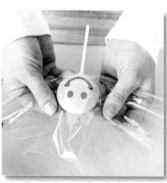

6 Make a small snip in the center of a cellophane square. Slide a smiley lollipop stick through the hole. Gently gather the corners of the cellophane up to the top of the lollipop, while creating a smooth appearance along the front of the pop and folding more cellophane towards the back. Secure the top with two pieces of rick-rack.

7 Clean and dry the can after removing the label and lid. If desired, cover any rough edges with duct tape. Trim Styrofoam to form a 3" tall cylinder shape to fit snugly inside the can. Cover Styrofoam with foil and insert into the can.

8 Place a rubber band around the center of the can. Hold the rubber band away from the can while inserting Pixy Stix between the band and the can. Work them into place in a semi-random color pattern; no glue or tape is needed. When satisfied with arrangement, cover the band with rick-rack and secure in the back with a straight pin.

9 Arrange lollipops by inserting sticks into Styrofoam. Trim sticks for shorter pops or add height by tightly taping shorter pieces of sticks to existing sticks. Fill the top of the base with Gobstopper candy.

Variation: Combine smile lollipops with candy of the same theme, such as "Jolly" Ranchers, Almond "Joy," "Snickers," "Chuckles," and "Laffy" Taffy.

Celebration Suggestions...

Congratulations, Get Well, Birthday or say, "You're an All-Star," "You Make Me Smile," or "Don't Worry, Be Happy!"

You Are My Sunshine

Sweets you will need:

- 1½ to 2 lbs. (approx. 250) Tootsie Roll Midgees for 1 sided bloom *or*
- 3 to 3½ lbs. (approx. 475) Tootsie Roll Midgees for 2 sided bloom

Supplies you will need:

- 1 (4″) Styrofoam ball
- Sharp knife
- Butter knife
- 18 (15 x 15″) pcs. yellow cellophane
- 1 (18″ long) ⅝ or ⅞″ dowel, painted green

- Straight pins
- Styrofoam (for base)
- Natural or painted clay pot (6″ diameter, 5¾″ tall)
- 10 (8 x 8″) pcs. green cellophane

To Begin...

1 With a sharp knife, score two lines, around the circumference of the ball, making them ½″ deep, and placing them ½″ apart. (Cuts have been marked with black marker for illustration purposes only.)

2 Pinch the center of a yellow cellophane square with fingers of one hand. Form a loop around the pinched end with the middle finger and thumb of the opposite hand; gently slide the looped fingers along the cellophane to gather it.

3 Flatten the tip of the gathered cellophane; lay the cellophane against the ball so the tip extends 2″ beyond the scored cut closest to you. Using the butter knife, poke the cellophane into the scored cut closest to you, until it is secure and just the very tip of gathered cellophane shows. This tip should face the other scored line so when the 2 rows of cellophane are complete, the tips are hidden

continued

45

between them. Continue by inserting additional pieces of gathered cellophane into the same scored cut, about every 1¼″. Use 9 pieces of cellophane for the first row.

4 In the same manner, make the second row of petals using 8 squares of cellophane, inserting them in the remaining scored cut. Leave space for the stem and final petal.

5 In the empty space, insert the dowel approximately 1″ into the ball; remove dowel until step 9 and set aside with last piece of cellophane.

6 Poke a pin through the twisted end of a Tootsie Roll wrapper; insert the pin into the Styrofoam ball next to the cellophane. Continue to densely add Tootsie Rolls by pinning through the previously pinned wrappers ends. When the first side is completely covered, fill the other side for a two-sided bloom, if desired.

7 Gather the reserved piece of cellophane as before, and tuck the tip into the previously started dowel hole. Re-insert the dowel next to the cellophane and carefully push the dowel to a depth of 1½″ to 2″, securing the dowel and the cellophane square.

8 Trim base Styrofoam to fit very snugly into the pot. Fold a piece of green cellophane in half and then half again; fan slightly and poke folded point down between the pot and the Styrofoam with a butter knife. Continue to poke cellophane around the entire edge of the pot about every 2½″ (takes about 7 pieces).

9 Insert the dowel (stem) of the flower into the Styrofoam base by pressing firmly and pushing it as deep as possible. Crumple remaining pieces of green cellophane and tuck in near the stem to cover any visible Styrofoam.

Tip: Pins can be dangerous when used near food. Inform guests or recipients to use caution as they enjoy this sweet arrangement. Suggest unwrapping the candy while still pinned to the ball, without removing the pin or wrapper. This will also allow the bloom to maintain a more attractive appearance as it is enjoyed.

Variation: Sprinkle wrapped candies on top of crumpled cellophane to offer additional sweet selections.

Celebration Suggestions...

Mother's Day, Garden Party, Farewell, Housewarming, or Tootsie Roll-Lover's Birthday! Say, "Your Future Looks Bright" or "Congrats on Your Golden Opportunity!"

Poppin'
Hydrangeas

Sweets you will need:

"Best Ever" Easy Popcorn Balls

- 5 qts. popped popcorn
- ¼ C. margarine
- ¾ C. light corn syrup
- 2 tsp. cold water
- 2½ C. powdered sugar
- 1 C. miniature marshmallows
- Gel food coloring (pink, green, purple, blue)

Supplies you will need:

- Basic cooking equipment for making popcorn balls
- Waxed paper
- Margarine for handling popcorn balls
- 15 (5-18″, 5-16″, 5-14″) ⅛″ wooden dowels or wooden skewers
- 10 C. sugar
- 2 (gal. size) zippered plastic bags
- Gel food coloring (purple)
- Glass cylinder vase (approx. 6″ diameter, 9″ tall)*
- 15 plastic faux leaves
- Petite clear rubberbands**

To Begin...

1 Divide popcorn evenly between 5 bowls. In a saucepan over medium heat, melt margarine, then add corn syrup, water, powdered sugar and marshmallows. Continually stir mixture as it heats to a rolling boil; continue to stir and boil for 3 minutes. Divide evenly between 5 separate microwave-safe bowls. Stir in coloring to create a variety of hues.

2 Pour 1 color of mixture over 1 bowl of popcorn. Stir to coat evenly. With clean, greased hands, quickly shape the coated popcorn into 3 balls and set aside on waxed paper. Repeat with remaining colors and popcorn. If corn syrup mixture begins to stiffen, reheat in microwave for 10 to 15 seconds to soften before stirring it into popcorn. Make 3 balls of 5 different colors for a total of 15.

3 Cut a 3″ square from waxed paper. Fold in half over the blunt tip of a wooden stem; roll the waxed paper ends around the stem end. Insert the waxed paper tip, not more than halfway, into the popcorn ball.*** Tightly pack the ball around the stem with clean greased hands. Repeat with remaining popcorn balls, making 3 differernt stem lengths of each color. Set them aside to harden for at least 1 hour.

4 If a colored sugar base is desired, divide white sugar evenly between two large zippered plastic bags. Add the gel food coloring of your choice to each bag, seal shut and work the color into the sugar. Use fingers to press and smooth out any clumps through the bag and/or add color until desired hue is reached. Combine the 2 bags of sugar and pour into the vase.

5 Wipe plastic leaves with a warm, damp, slightly soapy cloth; pat dry with paper towels. Loop rubber bands on leaf stems. Slide the looped bands onto the dowel, sliding the band and leaf upward to position it; vary height placement of the leaves as desired.

6 Arrange flowers in the vase by inserting dowel stems into the sugar. If desired, trim stems to more varied heights with a pruning shears.

*The size of vase can vary slightly; adjust amount of sugar and length of sticks as needed.

**Petite clear rubberbands are generally available in the hair accessory aisle of discount stores.

***Waxed paper is not edible, so it should remain partially visible and be removed before eating the popcorn ball.

Tip: *If popcorn balls need to be held for a length of time before service, after adding stems, wrap with clear plastic wrap and fasten around the stem with white twist ties or ribbon.*

Variation: *Color popcorn balls with thematic colors. For example, make red, white and blue flowers for a patriotic presentation.*

Celebration Suggestions...

Family Reunion, Anniversary Party, Birthday Party, Garden Party or a Housewarming Gift.

Harvest Sunset Wreath

Sweets you will need:

- **Approximately 1¼ lbs. butterscotch discs (96 pieces)**
- **Approximately 1⅛ lbs. cinnamon discs (80 pieces)**
- **5 (4 oz.) boxes Nips caramel flavored candy (80 pieces)**

Supplies you will need:

- 16 (12″) pcs. crafting wire
- Push pin or other sharp object
- 10″ solid foam wreath (outside measurement), 1½″ thick
- 30 x 1″ red ribbon (or coordinating color)
- 30 x 1½″ brown ribbon (or coordinating color)

To Begin...

1 Insert a piece of crafting wire through the twisted end of a butterscotch disc candy; slide candy onto the wire. Continue until 6 wires each hold 16 butterscotch discs. Repeat process with cinnamon disc candy until 5 wires each hold 16 cinnamon discs; then repeat process with Nips candies until 5 wires each hold 16 Nips. If necessary, poke a lead hole into the wrapper with a push pin before sliding candy onto the wire.

2 Slide butterscotch candies tightly together on one of the wires. Working carefully to keep the candies at the "front" of the wreath, bring the wire ends around to the "back" of the wreath; pull as tightly as possible and twist wires together to secure in place.

3 Wind loose wire ends loosely around a finger to form a little loop; press it flat against back of wreath. (By leaving longer ends, wires can be re-tightened if necessary.)

4 Alternating colors, continue to secure wired candy to wreath form until all candy has been secured. (The last wire of butterscotch discs will meet up with the first wire of butterscotch discs.)

5 Place red ribbon on top of brown ribbon, loop it through the wreath between the two side-by-side bundles of butterscotch candies, tie loose ends into a knot and trim ribbon ends as necessary. Hang so ribbon lies between butterscotch bundles.

Variation: Create a holiday wreath using green and red disc candies, or a patriotic wreath using red and white candies tied with a blue ribbon.

Celebration Suggestions...

Thanksgiving, Harvest Party, Halloween or another season using different candy colors.

Over the Hill?
Let's Just Say Retro

Sweets you will need:

- 2 flat taffy strips (McGraw's Confections)
- 1 Hershey's Mr. Goodbar
- 1 Hershey's Milk Chocolate Bar with Almonds
- 6 to 8 small Mary Jane candies
- 6 to 8 Bit-O-Honey candies
- 6 to 8 small Chick-O-Stick candies

- 1 Chuckles jelly candy package
- 1 Charleston Chew
- 1 5th Avenue candy bar
- 1 Necco Wafers roll
- 1 Pearson's Nut Goodie
- 1 GooGoo Supreme

- 2 old record albums
- Utility knife
- Styrofoam piece, (approximately 5 x 3 x 2")
- High-temperature glue gun
- Double stick tape
- Slinky toy
- Clear tape
- Low-temperature glue gun
- 18 to 24 (¼ x 5½") colored (or natural) wood craft sticks
- 5 to 10 black dominoes

To Begin...

1 From the outside edge of one record album, measure inward 4" and make a mark with the utility knife. Using the 4" mark and a solid straight edge as your guide, score a line across the album with the utility knife. Place the scored line along the edge of a solid surface; carefully place pressure on both sides of the album until it snaps into 2 pieces. Discard the smaller piece.

2 Lay the remaining whole album flat as the base for the arrangement. Position the cut piece of the album upright so the cut edge is against the base and the outside edges of the two albums match up. Hold the album in place and position the Styrofoam behind it as a prop; lay Styrofoam flat. When correctly positioned, use the high-temperature hot glue gun to secure the Styrofoam to the base album. Then hot glue the cut album to the Styrofoam, as the backdrop for the arrangement.

3 Secure one taffy against the backdrop album, along the back seam at a slight upwards angle, with double stick tape. Secure second taffy, in front of the first along the bottom of the base. On the right side, stand Mr. Goodbar and the Hershey's Milk Chocolate with Almonds upright against the backdrop and secure with double stick tape.

4 Place a "bent over" slinky on the left side of the base, approximately 1″ in front of the backdrop. Attach the two "rounds" of the slinky to the base album with clear tape. Using the low-temperature hot glue gun, place a small amount of glue on the end of a colored craft stick and secure a Mary Jane candy to the end of the stick. Repeat with remaining Mary Jane candies, Bit-O-Honey candies, and Chick-O-Stick candies. Slide stick ends through the slinky to arrange candy as desired.

5 Prop Chuckles, Charleston Chew, 5th Avenue bar and Necco Wafers roll upright behind the slinky; secure each to the backdrop with double stick tape.

6 Tuck Nut Goodie and GooGoo Supreme in front of Mr. Goodbar and Hershey's with Almonds; if desired, secure them with double stick tape.

7 Arrange stacked dominoes along the front; attach with double stick tape. If desired, use high-temp hot glue gun to attach 2 to 3 dominoes to the top of the backdrop album.

Tip: To secure items more tightly, use a low-temperature hot glue gun in place of tape.

Variation: Add white vinyl letters to the upright album with the words "Over the Hill," the recipient's name, or a message of your choice.

Additional Retro Candy Ideas:

Slim Jim	**Life Savers**
Saltwater taffy	**Chiclets**
Mallow Cups	**Goobers**
Root beer barrels	**Sugar Daddy**
Beemans gum	**Bun bar**
Clark Bar	**Old-fashioned candy sticks**
Oh Henry!	

Celebration Suggestions...

Birthday, Class Reunion, Family Reunion, Retirement or '50s-Theme Party

Visions of Gumdrops

Sweets you will need:

- 1 batch colorful* Crispy Marshmallow Treats (recipe on p. 5)
- 1 (32 oz.) cont. Spearmint Leaves (gumdrops)
- 1 (17 oz.) pkg. Spice Drops

Supplies you will need:

- 1 bowl measuring approx. ¾ to 1½″ larger than glass cylinder
- Margarine for handling cereal bars
- 1 (12″ to 13″) glass platter
- Food handling gloves, optional
- Toothpicks
- 1 (4″ to 5″) cylinder glass vase/candle holder
- 1 (2″ to 3″) pillar candle, or taper candle in a holder

To Begin...

1 Grease the outside upper portion of the bowl with margarine. Turn bowl upside down in the center of the glass platter. Mix one batch of Crispy Marshmallow Treats; spread mixture onto the platter, around the outside of the bowl. With margarine, grease food handling gloves or clean hands. Form cereal to shape a wreath base; leave a narrow edge around the outside of the platter and mound cereal up around the bowl. Gently remove bowl to leave the center of the platter open.

2 Stick a toothpick into the back side of a spearmint leaf until it almost pokes through the front side. Insert the toothpick into the cereal wreath's top edge while gently holding the inside of the wreath with lightly greased fingers. Continue to insert leaves in the same manner until the top ring of leaves is complete.

3 Poke a toothpick into the flat side of a spice drop until it almost pokes through the top. Insert the toothpick into the cereal wreath. Continue to poke leaves and drops, arranging in a random pattern, until wreath is complete.

4 Set glass cylinder and candle in the center of the wreath.

* Fruit crisps were the colorful cereal used in this recipe.

Celebration Suggestions...

Christmas Dinner, Hostess Gift, Holiday Office Party, or just say, "Merry Christmas!"